KU-526-572

Some stories from the gospel

The numbers in heavy type are page numbers.

Some of Jesus' miracles

Some of Jesus' teaching about...

JOHN

GOOD NEWS GOSPEL

THE BIBLE SOCIETIES/COLLINS

JOHN
GOOD NEWS GOSPEL

The Bible Societies/Collins, a division of HarperCollins*Publishers*

First edition published 1976
Second edition © 1994
This edition © 2005

Text, illustrations and all helps are copyright
Anglicised text © the British and Foreign Bible Society 1976, 1994, 2004
New Testament © American Bible Society 1966, 1971, 1976, 1992
Maps © United Bible Societies 1976, 1978

Title	Code	ISBN
John's Gospel	*GNB 560P JN*	*978 0 00 719349 3*
paperback pack of 10		

Typeset in FrutigerNext 9.5/11pt
using Corel Ventura 10 by
Solidus www.solid-us.com

Printed and bound in Great Britain
by Clays Ltd, St Ives plc

Use of up to 1000 verses from the *Good News Bible* is free, provided that they do not comprise a whole book, nor more than 50% of the work. Include this copyright notice: "Scriptures [marked GNB] are taken from the *Good News Bible* published by The Bible Societies/Collins © American Bible Society". For full information, go to www.biblesociety.org.uk/copyright.

The British and Foreign Bible Society is a member of the United Bible Societies which is a worldwide fellowship of National Bible Societies working in more than 180 countries. Their aim is to achieve the widest possible, effective and meaningful distribution of the Holy Scriptures, and to help people interact with the Word of God. More than 500 million Scriptures are distributed every year. You are invited to share in this work by your prayers and gifts. The Bible Society in your country will be very happy to provide details of its activity.

JERUSALEM IN NEW TESTAMENT TIMES

To Caesarea

Present City Wall

To Jericho

Damascus Gate

Pool of Bethzatha

PRAETORIUM

FORT

Ancient City Wall

To Bethany

TEMPLE

Gethsemane

Golgotha

Gate

Beautiful Gate

Gate

Court of Gentiles

Solomon's Porch

To Joppa

Gate

Gennath Gate

To Bethlehem

Bridge

Gates

HEROD'S PALACE

Pool

Present City Wall

KIDRON VALLEY

Pool of Siloam

0   200   400

Metres

Gate

Roads

VALLEY OF HINNOM

To Dead Sea

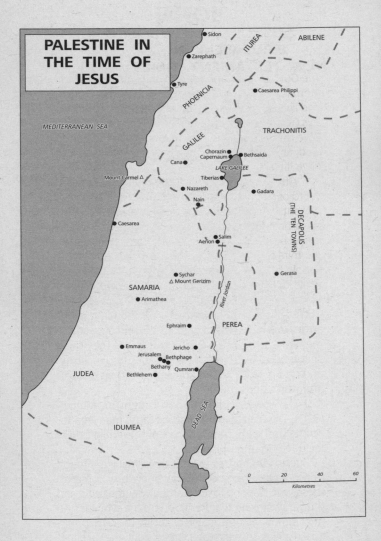

PALESTINE IN THE TIME OF JESUS

MEDITERRANEAN SEA

Sidon

Zarephath

Tyre

PHOENICIA

ITUREA

ABILENE

Caesarea Philippi

GALILEE

TRACHONITIS

Chorazin
Capernaum
Bethsaida

Cana

LAKE GALILEE

Mount Carmel △

Tiberias

Nazareth

Gadara

Nain

DECAPOLIS
(THE TEN TOWNS)

Caesarea

Salim
Aenon

Sychar
△ Mount Gerizim

Gerasa

SAMARIA

Arimathea

River Jordan

Ephraim

PEREA

Emmaus

Jericho

Jerusalem
Bethphage
Bethany

Qumran

JUDEA

Bethlehem

DEAD SEA

IDUMEA

0   20   40   60

Kilometres

THE GOSPEL ACCORDING TO
JOHN

INTRODUCTION

The Gospel according to John presents Jesus as the eternal Word of God, who "became a human being and lived among us." (1.14) As the book itself says, this Gospel was written so that its readers might believe that Jesus is the promised Saviour, the Son of God, and that through their faith in him they might have life (20.31).

After an introduction that identifies the eternal Word of God with Jesus, the first part of the Gospel presents various miracles which show that Jesus is the promised Saviour, the Son of God. These are followed by discourses that explain what is revealed by the miracles. This part of the book tells how some people believed in Jesus and became his followers, while others opposed him and refused to believe. Chapters 13—17 record at length the close fellowship of Jesus with his disciples on the night of his arrest, and his words of preparation and encouragement to them on the eve of his crucifixion. The closing chapters tell of Jesus' arrest and trial, his crucifixion and resurrection, and his appearances to his disciples after the resurrection.

The story of the woman caught in adultery (8.1–11) is placed in brackets because many manuscripts and early translations omit it, while others include it in other places.

John emphasizes the gift of eternal life through Christ, a gift which begins now and which comes to those who respond to Jesus as the way, the truth, and the life. A striking feature of *John* is the symbolic use of common things from everyday life to point to spiritual realities, such as water, bread, light, the shepherd and his sheep, and the grapevine and its fruit.

Outline of Contents

The Word of Life

1 In the beginning the Word already existed; the Word was with God, and the Word was God. 2 From the very beginning the Word was with God. 3 Through him God made all things; not one thing in all creation was made without him. 4 The Word was the source of life,* and this life brought light to humanity. 5 The light shines in the darkness, and the darkness has never put it out.

6 God sent his messenger, a man named John, 7 who came to tell people about the light, so that all should hear the message and believe. 8 He himself was not the light; he came to tell about the light. 9 This was the real light — the light that comes into the world and shines on everyone.

10 The Word was in the world, and though God made the world through him, yet the world did not recognize him. 11 He came to his own country, but his own people did not receive him. 12 Some, however, did receive him and believed in him; so he gave them the right to become God's children. 13 They did not become God's children by natural means, that is, by being born as the children of a human father; God himself was their Father.

14 The Word became a human being and, full of grace and truth, lived among us. We saw his glory, the glory which he received as the Father's only Son.

15 John spoke about him. He cried out, "This is the one I was talking about when I said, 'He comes after me, but he is greater than I am, because he existed before I was born.' "

1.4 The Word was the source of life; *or* What was made had life in union with the Word.

16 Out of the fullness of his grace he has blessed us all, giving us one blessing after another. 17 God gave the Law through Moses, but grace and truth came through Jesus Christ. 18 No one has ever seen God. The only Son, who is the same as God and is at the Father's side, he has made him known.

John the Baptist's Message
(Mt 3.1–12; Mk 1.1–8; Lk 3.1–18)

19 The Jewish authorities in Jerusalem sent some priests and Levites to John, to ask him, "Who are you?"

20 John did not refuse to answer, but spoke out openly and clearly, saying: "I am not the Messiah."

21 "Who are you, then?" they asked. "Are you Elijah?"

"No, I am not," John answered.

"Are you the Prophet?"* they asked.

"No," he replied.

22 "Then tell us who you are," they said. "We have to take an answer back to those who sent us. What do you say about yourself?"

23 John answered by quoting the prophet Isaiah:

"I am 'the voice of someone shouting in the desert:
    Make a straight path for the Lord to travel!' "

24 The messengers, who had been sent by the Pharisees, 25 then* asked John, "If you are not the Messiah nor Elijah nor the Prophet, why do you baptize?"

26 John answered, "I baptize with water, but among you stands the one you do not know. 27 He is coming after me, but I am not good enough even to untie his sandals."

28 All this happened in Bethany on the east side of the River Jordan, where John was baptizing.

The Lamb of God

29 The next day John saw Jesus coming to him, and said, "There is the Lamb of God, who takes away the sin of the world! 30 This is the one I was talking about when I said, 'A man is coming after me,

---

1.21 THE PROPHET: *The one who was expected to appear and announce the coming of the Messiah.*
1.25 The messengers, who had been sent by the Pharisees, then; *or* Those who had been sent were Pharisees; they.

but he is greater than I am, because he existed before I was born.'
31 I did not know who he would be, but I came baptizing with water in order to make him known to the people of Israel."

32 And John gave this testimony: "I saw the Spirit come down like a dove from heaven and stay on him. 33 I still did not know that he was the one, but God, who sent me to baptize with water, had said to me, 'You will see the Spirit come down and stay on a man; he is the one who baptizes with the Holy Spirit.' 34 I have seen it," said John, "and I tell you that he is the Son of God."

I saw the Spirit come down like a dove   (1.32)

The First Disciples of Jesus

35 The next day John was standing there again with two of his disciples, 36 when he saw Jesus walking by. "There is the Lamb of God!" he said.

37 The two disciples heard him say this and went with Jesus. 38 Jesus turned, saw them following him, and asked, "What are you looking for?"

They answered, "Where do you live, Rabbi?" (This word means "Teacher".)

³⁹ "Come and see," he answered. (It was then about four o'clock in the afternoon.) So they went with him and saw where he lived, and spent the rest of that day with him.

⁴⁰ One of them was Andrew, Simon Peter's brother. ⁴¹ At once he found his brother Simon and told him, "We have found the Messiah." (This word means "Christ".) ⁴² Then he took Simon to Jesus.

Jesus looked at him and said, "Your name is Simon son of John, but you will be called Cephas." (This is the same as Peter and means "a rock".)

Jesus Calls Philip and Nathanael

⁴³ The next day Jesus decided to go to Galilee. He found Philip and said to him, "Come with me!" ⁴⁴ (Philip was from Bethsaida, the town where Andrew and Peter lived.) ⁴⁵ Philip found Nathanael and told him, "We have found the one whom Moses wrote about in the book of the Law and whom the prophets also wrote about. He is Jesus son of Joseph, from Nazareth."

⁴⁶ "Can anything good come from Nazareth?" Nathanael asked.

"Come and see," answered Philip.

⁴⁷ When Jesus saw Nathanael coming to him, he said about him, "Here is a real Israelite; there is nothing false in him!"

⁴⁸ Nathanael asked him, "How do you know me?"

Jesus answered, "I saw you when you were under the fig tree before Philip called you."

⁴⁹ "Teacher," answered Nathanael, "you are the Son of God! You are the King of Israel!"

⁵⁰ Jesus said, "Do you believe just because I told you I saw you when you were under the fig tree? You will see much greater things than this!" ⁵¹ And he said to them, "I am telling you the truth: you will see heaven open and God's angels going up and coming down on the Son of Man."

The Wedding in Cana

2 Two days later there was a wedding in the town of Cana in Galilee. Jesus' mother was there, ² and Jesus and his disciples had also been invited to the wedding. ³ When the wine had given out, Jesus' mother said to him, "They have no wine left."

Fill these jars with water (2.7)

4 "You must not tell me what to do," Jesus replied. "My time has not yet come."

5 Jesus' mother then told the servants, "Do whatever he tells you."

6 The Jews have rules about ritual washing, and for this purpose six stone water jars were there, each one large enough to hold about a hundred litres. 7 Jesus said to the servants, "Fill these jars with water." They filled them to the brim, 8 and then he told them, "Now draw some water out and take it to the man in charge of the feast." They took him the water, 9 which now had turned into wine, and he tasted it. He did not know where this wine had come from (but, of course, the servants who had drawn out the water knew); so he called the bridegroom 10 and said to him, "Everyone else serves the best wine first, and after the guests have had plenty to drink, he serves the ordinary wine. But you have kept the best wine until now!"

11 Jesus performed this first miracle in Cana in Galilee; there he revealed his glory, and his disciples believed in him.

12 After this, Jesus and his mother, brothers, and disciples went to Capernaum and stayed there a few days.

Jesus Goes to the Temple

(Mt 21.12–13; Mk 11.15–17; Lk 19.45–46)

13 It was almost time for the Passover Festival, so Jesus went to Jerusalem. 14 There in the Temple he found people selling cattle, sheep, and pigeons, and also the moneychangers sitting at their tables. 15 So he made a whip from cords and drove all the animals out of the Temple, both the sheep and the cattle; he overturned the tables of the moneychangers and scattered their coins; 16 and he ordered those who sold the pigeons, "Take them out of here! Stop making my Father's house a market place!" 17 His disciples remembered that the scripture says, "My devotion to your house, O God, burns in me like a fire."

18 The Jewish authorities replied with a question, "What miracle can you perform to show us that you have the right to do this?"

19 Jesus answered, "Tear down this Temple, and in three days I will build it again."

20 "Are you going to build it again in three days?" they asked him. "It has taken forty-six years to build this Temple!"

21 But the temple Jesus was speaking about was his body. 22 So when he was raised from death, his disciples remembered that he had said this, and they believed the scripture and what Jesus had said.

Jesus' Knowledge of Human Nature

23 While Jesus was in Jerusalem during the Passover Festival, many believed in him as they saw the miracles he performed. 24 But Jesus did not trust himself to them, because he knew them all. 25 There was no need for anyone to tell him about them, because he himself knew what was in their hearts.

Jesus and Nicodemus

3 There was a Jewish leader named Nicodemus, who belonged to the party of the Pharisees. 2 One night he went to Jesus and said to him, "Rabbi, we know that you are a teacher sent by God. No one could perform the miracles you are doing unless God were with him."

3 Jesus answered, "I am telling you the truth: no one can see the Kingdom of God without being born again."*

3.3, 3.7 again; *or* from above.

4 "How can a grown man be born again?" Nicodemus asked. "He certainly cannot enter his mother's womb and be born a second time!"

5 "I am telling you the truth," replied Jesus. "No one can enter the Kingdom of God without being born of water and the Spirit. 6 A person is born physically of human parents, but is born spiritually of the Spirit. 7 Do not be surprised because I tell you that you must all be born again.* 8 The wind blows wherever it wishes; you hear the sound it makes, but you do not know where it comes from or where it is going. It is like that with everyone who is born of the Spirit."

9 "How can this be?" asked Nicodemus.

10 Jesus answered, "You are a great teacher in Israel, and you don't know this? 11 I am telling you the truth: we speak of what we know and report what we have seen, yet none of you is willing to accept our message. 12 You do not believe me when I tell you about the things of this world; how will you ever believe me, then, when I tell you about the things of heaven? 13 And no one has ever gone up to heaven except the Son of Man, who came down from heaven."*

14 As Moses lifted up the bronze snake on a pole in the desert, in the same way the Son of Man must be lifted up, 15 so that everyone who believes in him may have eternal life. 16 For God loved the world so much that he gave his only Son, so that everyone who believes in him may not die but have eternal life. 17 For God did not send his Son into the world to be its judge, but to be its saviour.

18 Those who believe in the Son are not judged; but those who do not believe have already been judged, because they have not believed in God's only Son. 19 This is how the judgement works: the light has come into the world, but people love the darkness rather than the light, because their deeds are evil. 20 All those who do evil things hate the light and will not come to the light, because they do not want their evil deeds to be shown up. 21 But those who do what is true come to the light in order that the light may show that what they did was in obedience to God.

3.7, 3.3 again; *or* from above.
3.13 *The quotation may continue through verse 21.*

Jesus and John

22 After this, Jesus and his disciples went to the province of Judea, where he spent some time with them and baptized. 23 John also was baptizing in Aenon, not far from Salim, because there was plenty of water in that place. People were going to him, and he was baptizing them. 24 (This was before John had been put in prison.)

25 Some of John's disciples began arguing with a Jew* about the matter of ritual washing. 26 So they went to John and said, "Teacher, you remember the man who was with you on the east side of the Jordan, the one you spoke about? Well, he is baptizing now, and everyone is going to him!"

27 John answered, "No one can have anything unless God gives it to him. 28 You yourselves are my witnesses that I said, 'I am not the Messiah, but I have been sent ahead of him.' 29 The bridegroom is the one to whom the bride belongs; but the bridegroom's friend, who stands by and listens, is glad when he hears the bridegroom's voice. This is how my own happiness is made complete. 30 He must become more important while I become less important."

He who Comes from Heaven

31 He who comes from above is greater than all. He who is from the earth belongs to the earth and speaks about earthly matters, but he who comes from heaven is above all. 32 He tells what he has seen and heard, yet no one accepts his message. 33 But whoever accepts his message confirms by this that God is truthful. 34 The one whom God has sent speaks God's words, because God gives him the fullness of his Spirit. 35 The Father loves his Son and has put everything in his power. 36 Whoever believes in the Son has eternal life; whoever disobeys the Son will not have life, but will remain under God's punishment.

Jesus and the Samaritan Woman

4 The Pharisees heard that Jesus was winning and baptizing more disciples than John. 2 (Actually, Jesus himself did not baptize anyone; only his disciples did.) 3 So when Jesus heard

---

3.25 a Jew; *some manuscripts have* some Jews.

what was being said, he left Judea and went back to Galilee;
4 on his way there he had to go through Samaria.

5 In Samaria he came to a town named Sychar, which was not far
from the field that Jacob had given to his son Joseph. 6 Jacob's
well was there, and Jesus, tired out by the journey, sat down by the
well. It was about noon.

7 A Samaritan woman came to draw some water, and Jesus said
to her, "Give me a drink of water." 8 (His disciples had gone into
town to buy food.)

Give me a drink of water   (4.7)

9 The woman answered, "You are a Jew, and I am a Samaritan —
so how can you ask me for a drink?" (Jews will not use the same
cups and bowls that Samaritans use.)*

10 Jesus answered, "If only you knew what God gives and who it
is that is asking you for a drink, you would ask him, and he would
give you life-giving water."

11 "Sir," the woman said, "you haven't got a bucket, and the well
is deep. Where would you get that life-giving water? 12 It was our
ancestor Jacob who gave us this well; he and his sons and his flocks
all drank from it. You don't claim to be greater than Jacob, do you?"

13 Jesus answered, "All those who drink this water will be thirsty
again, 14 but whoever drinks the water that I will give him will

---

4.9 Jews will not use the same cups and bowls that Samaritans use; *or* Jews will
have nothing to do with Samaritans.

never be thirsty again. The water that I will give him will become in him a spring which will provide him with life-giving water and give him eternal life."

15 "Sir," the woman said, "give me that water! Then I will never be thirsty again, nor will I have to come here to draw water."

16 "Go and call your husband," Jesus told her, "and come back."

17 "I haven't got a husband," she answered.

Jesus replied, "You are right when you say you haven't got a husband. 18 You have been married to five men, and the man you live with now is not really your husband. You have told me the truth."

19 "I see you are a prophet, sir," the woman said. 20 "My Samaritan ancestors worshipped God on this mountain, but you Jews say that Jerusalem is the place where we should worship God."

21 Jesus said to her, "Believe me, woman, the time will come when people will not worship the Father either on this mountain or in Jerusalem. 22 You Samaritans do not really know whom you worship; but we Jews know whom we worship, because it is from the Jews that salvation comes. 23 But the time is coming and is already here, when by the power of God's Spirit people will worship the Father as he really is, offering him the true worship that he wants. 24 God is Spirit, and only by the power of his Spirit can people worship him as he really is."

25 The woman said to him, "I know that the Messiah will come, and when he comes, he will tell us everything."

26 Jesus answered, "I am he, I who am talking with you."

27 At that moment Jesus' disciples returned, and they were greatly surprised to find him talking with a woman. But none of them said to her, "What do you want?" or asked him, "Why are you talking with her?"

28 Then the woman left her water jar, went back to the town, and said to the people there, 29 "Come and see the man who told me everything I have ever done. Could he be the Messiah?" 30 So they left the town and went to Jesus.

31 In the meantime the disciples were begging Jesus, "Teacher, have something to eat!"

32 But he answered, "I have food to eat that you know nothing about."

33 So the disciples started asking among themselves, "Could somebody have brought him food?"

34 "My food," Jesus said to them, "is to obey the will of the one who sent me and to finish the work he gave me to do. 35 You have a saying, 'Four more months and then the harvest.' But I tell you, take a good look at the fields; the crops are now ripe and ready to be harvested! 36 The one who reaps the harvest is being paid and gathers the crops for eternal life; so another who sows and the one who reaps will be glad together. 37 The saying is true, 'One sows, another reaps.' 38 I have sent you to reap a harvest in a field where you did not work; others worked there, and you profit from their work."

39 Many of the Samaritans in that town believed in Jesus because the woman had said, "He told me everything I have ever done." 40 So when the Samaritans came to him, they begged him to stay with them, and Jesus stayed there two days.

41 Many more believed because of his message, 42 and they said to the woman, "We believe now, not because of what you said, but because we ourselves have heard him, and we know that he really is the Saviour of the world."

Jesus Heals an Official's Son

43 After spending two days there, Jesus left and went to Galilee. 44 For he himself had said, "A prophet is not respected in his own country." 45 When he arrived in Galilee, the people there welcomed him, because they had gone to the Passover Festival in Jerusalem and had seen everything that he had done during the festival.

46 Then Jesus went back to Cana in Galilee, where he had turned the water into wine. A government official was there whose son was ill in Capernaum. 47 When he heard that Jesus had come from Judea to Galilee, he went to him and asked him to go to Capernaum and heal his son, who was about to die. 48 Jesus said to him, "None of you will ever believe unless you see miracles and wonders."

49 "Sir," replied the official, "come with me before my child dies." 50 Jesus said to him, "Go, your son will live!"

The man believed Jesus' words and went. 51 On his way home his servants met him with the news, "Your boy is going to live!"

52 He asked them what time it was when his son got better, and they answered, "It was one o'clock yesterday afternoon when the fever left him." 53 Then the father remembered it was at that

very hour that Jesus had told him, "Your son will live." So he and all his family believed.

⁵⁴ This was the second miracle that Jesus performed after coming from Judea to Galilee.

The Healing at the Pool

5 After this, Jesus went to Jerusalem for a religious festival. ² Near the Sheep Gate in Jerusalem there is a pool* with five porches; in Hebrew it is called Bethzatha.* ³ A large crowd of sick people were lying in the porches — the blind, the lame, and the paralysed.* ⁵ A man was there who had been ill for 38 years. ⁶ Jesus saw him lying there, and he knew that the man had been ill for such a long time; so he asked him, "Do you want to get well?"

⁷ The sick man answered, "Sir, I have no one here to put me in the pool when the water is stirred up; while I am trying to get in, somebody else gets there first."

⁸ Jesus said to him, "Get up, pick up your mat, and walk." ⁹ Immediately the man got well; he picked up his mat and started walking.

The day this happened was a Sabbath, ¹⁰ so the Jewish authorities told the man who had been healed, "This is a Sabbath, and it is against our Law for you to carry your mat."

¹¹ He answered, "The man who made me well told me to pick up my mat and walk."

¹² They asked him, "Who is the man who told you to do this?"

¹³ But the man who had been healed did not know who Jesus was, for there was a crowd in that place, and Jesus had slipped away.

¹⁴ Afterwards, Jesus found him in the Temple and said, "Listen, you are well now; so stop sinning or something worse may happen to you."

¹⁵ Then the man left and told the Jewish authorities that it was Jesus who had healed him. ¹⁶ So they began to persecute Jesus,

---

5.2 Near the Sheep Gate... a pool; *or* Near the Sheep Pool... a place.
5.2 Bethzatha; *some manuscripts have* Bethesda.
5.3 *Some manuscripts add verses 3b–4:* They were waiting for the water to move, ⁴ because every now and then an angel of the Lord went down into the pool and stirred up the water. The first sick person to go into the pool after the water was stirred up was healed from whatever disease he had.

because he had done this healing on a Sabbath. 17 Jesus answered them, "My Father is always working, and I too must work."

18 This saying made the Jewish authorities all the more determined to kill him; not only had he broken the Sabbath law, but he had said that God was his own Father and in this way had made himself equal with God.

The Authority of the Son

19 So Jesus answered them, "I am telling you the truth: the Son can do nothing on his own; he does only what he sees his Father doing. What the Father does, the Son also does. 20 For the Father loves the Son and shows him all that he himself is doing. He will show him even greater things to do than this, and you will all be amazed. 21 Just as the Father raises the dead and gives them life, in the same way the Son gives life to those he wants to. 22 Nor does the Father himself judge anyone. He has given his Son the full right to judge, 23 so that all will honour the Son in the same way as they honour the Father. Whoever does not honour the Son does not honour the Father who sent him.

24 "I am telling you the truth: those who hear my words and believe in him who sent me have eternal life. They will not be judged, but have already passed from death to life. 25 I am telling you the truth: the time is coming — the time has already come — when the dead will hear the voice of the Son of God, and those who hear it will come to life. 26 Just as the Father is himself the source of life, in the same way he has made his Son to be the source of life. 27 And he has given the Son the right to judge, because he is the Son of Man. 28 Do not be surprised at this; the time is coming when all the dead will hear his voice 29 and come out of their graves: those who have done good will rise and live, and those who have done evil will rise and be condemned.

Witnesses to Jesus

30 "I can do nothing on my own authority; I judge only as God tells me, so my judgement is right, because I am not trying to do what I want, but only what he who sent me wants.

31 "If I testify on my own behalf, what I say is not to be accepted as real proof. 32 But there is someone else who testifies on my behalf, and I know that what he says about me is true. 33 John is the one to whom you sent your messengers, and he spoke on behalf of the

truth. 34 It is not that I must have a human witness; I say this only in order that you may be saved. 35 John was like a lamp, burning and shining, and you were willing for a while to enjoy his light. 36 But I have a witness on my behalf which is even greater than the witness that John gave: what I do, that is, the deeds my Father gave me to do, these speak on my behalf and show that the Father has sent me. 37 And the Father, who sent me, also testifies on my behalf. You have never heard his voice or seen his face, 38 and you do not keep his message in your hearts, for you do not believe in the one whom he sent. 39 You study the Scriptures, because you think that in them you will find eternal life. And these very Scriptures speak about me! 40 Yet you are not willing to come to me in order to have life.

41 "I am not looking for human praise. 42 But I know what kind of people you are, and I know that you have no love for God in your hearts. 43 I have come with my Father's authority, but you have not received me; when, however, someone comes with his own authority, you will receive him. 44 You like to receive praise from one another, but you do not try to win praise from the one who alone is God; how, then, can you believe me? 45 Do not think, however, that I am the one who will accuse you to my Father. Moses, in whom you have put your hope, is the very one who will accuse you. 46 If you had really believed Moses, you would have believed me, because he wrote about me. 47 But since you do not believe what he wrote, how can you believe what I say?"

Jesus Feeds a Great Crowd
(Mt 14.13–21; Mk 6.30–44; Lk 9.10–17)

6 After this, Jesus went across Lake Galilee (or, Lake Tiberias, as it is also called). 2 A large crowd followed him, because they had seen his miracles of healing those who were ill. 3 Jesus went up a hill and sat down with his disciples. 4 The time for the Passover Festival was near. 5 Jesus looked round and saw that a large crowd was coming to him, so he asked Philip, "Where can we buy enough food to feed all these people?" 6 (He said this to test Philip; actually he already knew what he would do.)

7 Philip answered, "For everyone to have even a little, it would take more than two hundred silver coins* to buy enough bread."

6.7 SILVER COINS: *A silver coin was the daily wage of a rural worker (see Mt 20.2).*

8 Another of his disciples, Andrew, who was Simon Peter's brother, said, 9 "There is a boy here who has five loaves of barley bread and two fish. But they will certainly not be enough for all these people."

10 "Make the people sit down," Jesus told them. (There was a lot of grass there.) So all the people sat down; there were about 5,000 men. 11 Jesus took the bread, gave thanks to God, and distributed it to the people who were sitting there. He did the same with the fish, and they all had as much as they wanted. 12 When they were all full, he said to his disciples, "Gather the pieces left over; let us not waste any." 13 So they gathered them all up and filled twelve baskets with the pieces left over from the five barley loaves which the people had eaten.

14 Seeing this miracle that Jesus had performed, the people there said, "Surely this is the Prophet* who was to come into the world!" 15 Jesus knew that they were about to come and seize him in order to make him king by force; so he went off again to the hills by himself.

Jesus Walks on the Water
(Mt 14.22–33; Mk 6.45–52)
16 When evening came, Jesus' disciples went down to the lake, 17 got into a boat, and went back across the lake towards Capernaum. Night came on, and Jesus still had not come to them. 18 By then a strong wind was blowing and stirring up the water. 19 The disciples had rowed about five or six kilometres when they saw Jesus walking on the water, coming near the boat, and they were terrified. 20 "Don't be afraid," Jesus told them, "it is I!" 21 Then they willingly took him into the boat, and immediately the boat reached land at the place they were heading for.

The People Seek Jesus
22 Next day the crowd which had stayed on the other side of the lake realized that there had been only one boat there. They knew that Jesus had not gone in it with his disciples, but that they had left without him. 23 Other boats, which were from Tiberias, came to shore near the place where the crowd had eaten the bread

---

6.14 THE PROPHET: *See 1.21.*

after the Lord had given thanks. 24 When the crowd saw that Jesus was not there, nor his disciples, they got into those boats and went to Capernaum, looking for him.

Jesus the Bread of Life

25 When the people found Jesus on the other side of the lake, they said to him, "Teacher, when did you get here?"

26 Jesus answered, "I am telling you the truth: you are looking for me because you ate the bread and had all you wanted, not because you understood my miracles. 27 Do not work for food that goes bad; instead, work for the food that lasts for eternal life. This is the food which the Son of Man will give you, because God, the Father, has put his mark of approval on him."

28 So they asked him, "What can we do in order to do what God wants us to do?"

29 Jesus answered, "What God wants you to do is to believe in the one he sent."

30 They replied, "What miracle will you perform so that we may see it and believe you? What will you do? 31 Our ancestors ate manna in the desert, just as the scripture says, 'He gave them bread from heaven to eat.' "

32 "I am telling you the truth," Jesus said. "What Moses gave you was not* the bread from heaven; it is my Father who gives you the real bread from heaven. 33 For the bread that God gives is he who comes down from heaven and gives life to the world."

34 "Sir," they asked him, "give us this bread always."

35 "I am the bread of life," Jesus told them. "Those who come to me will never be hungry; those who believe in me will never be thirsty. 36 Now, I told you that you have seen me but will not believe. 37 Everyone whom my Father gives me will come to me. I will never turn away anyone who comes to me, 38 because I have come down from heaven to do not my own will but the will of him who sent me. 39 And it is the will of him who sent me that I should not lose any of all those he has given me, but that I should raise them all to life on the last day. 40 For what my Father wants is that all who see the Son and believe in him should have eternal life. And I will raise them to life on the last day."

6.32 What Moses gave you was not; *or* It was not Moses who gave you.

41 The people started grumbling about him, because he said, "I am the bread that came down from heaven." 42 So they said, "This man is Jesus son of Joseph, isn't he? We know his father and mother. How, then, does he now say he came down from heaven?"

43 Jesus answered, "Stop grumbling among yourselves. 44 No one can come to me unless the Father who sent me draws him to me; and I will raise him to life on the last day. 45 The prophets wrote, 'Everyone will be taught by God.' Anyone who hears the Father and learns from him comes to me. 46 This does not mean that anyone has seen the Father; he who is from God is the only one who has seen the Father. 47 I am telling you the truth: he who believes has eternal life. 48 I am the bread of life. 49 Your ancestors ate manna in the desert, but they died. 50 But the bread that comes down from heaven is of such a kind that whoever eats it will not die. 51 I am the living bread that came down from heaven. If anyone eats this bread, he will live for ever. The bread that I will give him is my flesh, which I give so that the world may live."

52 This started an angry argument among them. "How can this man give us his flesh to eat?" they asked.

53 Jesus said to them, "I am telling you the truth: if you do not eat the flesh of the Son of Man and drink his blood, you will not have life in yourselves. 54 Those who eat my flesh and drink my blood have eternal life, and I will raise them to life on the last day. 55 For my flesh is the real food; my blood is the real drink. 56 Those who eat my flesh and drink my blood live in me, and I live in them. 57 The living Father sent me, and because of him I live also. In the same way whoever eats me will live because of me. 58 This, then, is the bread that came down from heaven; it is not like the bread that your ancestors ate. They later died, but those who eat this bread will live for ever."

59 Jesus said this as he taught in the synagogue in Capernaum.

The Words of Eternal Life

60 Many of his followers heard this and said, "This teaching is too hard. Who can listen to it?"

61 Without being told, Jesus knew that they were grumbling about this, so he said to them, "Does this make you want to give up? 62 Suppose, then, that you should see the Son of Man go back

up to the place where he was before? 63 What gives life is God's Spirit; human power is of no use at all. The words I have spoken to you bring God's life-giving Spirit. 64 Yet some of you do not believe." (Jesus knew from the very beginning who were the ones that would not believe and which one would betray him.) 65 And he added, "This is the very reason I told you that no one can come to me unless the Father makes it possible for him to do so."

66 Because of this, many of Jesus' followers turned back and would not go with him any more. 67 So he asked the twelve disciples, "And you — would you also like to leave?"

68 Simon Peter answered him, "Lord, to whom would we go? You have the words that give eternal life. 69 And now we believe and know that you are the Holy One who has come from God."

70 Jesus replied, "I chose the twelve of you, didn't I? Yet one of you is a devil!" 71 He was talking about Judas, the son of Simon Iscariot. For Judas, even though he was one of the twelve disciples, was going to betray him.

Jesus and his Brothers

7 After this, Jesus travelled in Galilee; he did not want to travel in Judea, because the Jewish authorities there were wanting to kill him. 2 The time for the Festival of Shelters was near, 3 so Jesus' brothers said to him, "Leave this place and go to Judea, so that your followers will see the things that you are doing. 4 No one hides what he is doing if he wants to be well known. Since you are doing these things, let the whole world know about you!" 5 (Not even his brothers believed in him.)

6 Jesus said to them, "The right time for me has not yet come. Any time is right for you. 7 The world cannot hate you, but it hates me, because I keep telling it that its ways are bad. 8 You go on to the festival. I am not going* to this festival, because the right time has not come for me." 9 He said this, and then stayed on in Galilee.

Jesus at the Festival of Shelters

10 After his brothers had gone to the festival, Jesus also went; however, he did not go openly, but secretly. 11 The Jewish authorities were looking for him at the festival. "Where is he?" they asked.

7.8 I am not going; *some manuscripts have* I am not yet going.

12 There was much whispering about him in the crowd. "He is a good man," some people said. "No," others said, "he is misleading the people." 13 But no one talked about him openly, because they were afraid of the Jewish authorities.

14 The festival was nearly half over when Jesus went to the Temple and began teaching. 15 The Jewish authorities were greatly surprised and said, "How does this man know so much when he has never had any training?"

16 Jesus answered, "What I teach is not my own teaching, but it comes from God, who sent me. 17 Whoever is willing to do what God wants will know whether what I teach comes from God or whether I speak on my own authority. 18 A person who speaks on his own authority is trying to gain glory for himself. But he who wants glory for the one who sent him is honest, and there is nothing false in him. 19 Moses gave you the Law, didn't he? But not one of you obeys the Law. Why are you trying to kill me?"

20 "You have a demon in you!" the crowd answered. "Who is trying to kill you?"

21 Jesus answered, "I performed one miracle, and you were all surprised. 22 Moses ordered you to circumcise your sons (although it was not Moses but your ancestors who started it), and so you circumcise a boy on the Sabbath. 23 If a boy is circumcised on the Sabbath so that Moses' Law is not broken, why are you angry with me because I made a man completely well on the Sabbath? 24 Stop judging by external standards, and judge by true standards."

Is he the Messiah?

25 Some of the people of Jerusalem said, "Isn't this the man the authorities are trying to kill? 26 Look! He is talking in public, and they say nothing against him! Can it be that they really know that he is the Messiah? 27 But when the Messiah comes, no one will know where he is from. And we all know where this man comes from."

28 As Jesus taught in the Temple, he said in a loud voice, "Do you really know me and know where I am from? I have not come on my own authority. He who sent me, however, is truthful. You do not know him, 29 but I know him, because I come from him and he sent me."

30 Then they tried to seize him, but no one laid a hand on him, because his hour had not yet come. 31 But many in the crowd believed in him and said, "When the Messiah comes, will he perform more miracles than this man has?"

Guards are Sent to Arrest Jesus

32 The Pharisees heard the crowd whispering these things about Jesus, so they and the chief priests sent some guards to arrest him. 33 Jesus said, "I shall be with you a little while longer, and then I shall go away to him who sent me. 34 You will look for me, but you will not find me, because you cannot go where I will be."

35 The Jewish authorities said among themselves, "Where is he about to go so that we shall not find him? Will he go to the Greek cities where our people live, and teach the Greeks? 36 He says that we will look for him but will not find him, and that we cannot go where he will be. What does he mean?"

Streams of Life-giving Water

37 On the last and most important day of the festival Jesus stood up and said in a loud voice, "Whoever is thirsty should come to me, and 38 whoever believes in me should drink. As the scripture says, 'Streams of life-giving water will pour out from his side.' "* 39 Jesus said this about the Spirit, which those who believed in him were going to receive. At that time the Spirit had not yet been given, because Jesus had not been raised to glory.

Division among the People

40 Some of the people in the crowd heard him say this and said, "This man is really the Prophet!"*

41 Others said, "He is the Messiah!"

But others said, "The Messiah will not come from Galilee! 42 The scripture says that the Messiah will be a descendant of King David and will be born in Bethlehem, the town where David lived." 43 So there was a division in the crowd because of Jesus. 44 Some wanted to seize him, but no one laid a hand on him.

7.38 *Jesus' words in verses 37–38 may be translated:* "Whoever is thirsty should come to me and drink. 38 As the scripture says, 'Streams of life-giving water will pour out from within anyone who believes in me.' "
7.40 THE PROPHET: *See 1.21.*

The Unbelief of the Jewish Authorities

45 When the guards went back, the chief priests and Pharisees asked them, "Why did you not bring him?"

46 The guards answered, "Nobody has ever talked like this man!"

47 "Did he fool you, too?" the Pharisees asked them. 48 "Have you ever known one of the authorities or one Pharisee to believe in him? 49 This crowd does not know the Law of Moses, so they are under God's curse!"

50 One of the Pharisees there was Nicodemus, the man who had gone to see Jesus before. He said to the others, 51 "According to our Law we cannot condemn anyone before hearing him and finding out what he has done."

52 "Well," they answered, "are you also from Galilee? Study the Scriptures and you will learn that no prophet ever comes* from Galilee."

The Woman Caught in Adultery

8 [Then everyone went home, but Jesus went to the Mount of Olives. 2 Early the next morning he went back to the Temple. All the people gathered round him, and he sat down and began to teach them. 3 The teachers of the Law and the Pharisees brought in a woman who had been caught committing adultery, and they made her stand before them all. 4 "Teacher," they said to Jesus, "this woman was caught in the very act of committing adultery. 5 In our Law Moses commanded that such a woman must be stoned to death. Now, what do you say?" 6 They said this to trap Jesus, so that they could accuse him. But he bent over and wrote on the ground with his finger.

7 As they stood there asking him questions, he straightened himself up and said to them, "Whichever one of you has committed no sin may throw the first stone at her." 8 Then he bent over again and wrote on the ground. 9 When they heard this, they all left, one by one, the older ones first. Jesus was left alone, with the woman still standing there. 10 He straightened himself up and said to her, "Where are they? Is there no one left to condemn you?"

7.52 no prophet ever comes; *one manuscript has* the Prophet will not come.

11 "No one, sir," she answered.

"Well, then," Jesus said, "I do not condemn you either. Go, but do not sin again."]*

Jesus the Light of the World

12 Jesus spoke to the Pharisees again. "I am the light of the world," he said. "Whoever follows me will have the light of life and will never walk in darkness."

13 The Pharisees said to him, "Now you are testifying on your own behalf; what you say proves nothing."

14 "No," Jesus answered, "even though I do testify on my own behalf, what I say is true, because I know where I came from and where I am going. You do not know where I came from or where I am going. 15 You make judgements in a purely human way; I pass judgement on no one. 16 But if I were to do so, my judgement would be true, because I am not alone in this; the Father who sent me is with me. 17 It is written in your Law that when two witnesses agree, what they say is true. 18 I testify on my own behalf, and the Father who sent me also testifies on my behalf."

19 "Where is your father?" they asked him.

"You know neither me nor my Father," Jesus answered. "If you knew me, you would know my Father also."

20 Jesus said all this as he taught in the Temple, in the room where the offering boxes were placed. And no one arrested him, because his hour had not come.

You cannot Go Where I am Going

21 Again Jesus said to them, "I will go away; you will look for me, but you will die in your sins. You cannot go where I am going."

22 So the Jewish authorities said, "He says that we cannot go where he is going. Does this mean that he will kill himself?"

23 Jesus answered, "You belong to this world here below, but I come from above. You are from this world, but I am not from this world. 24 That is why I told you that you will die in your sins. And you will die in your sins if you do not believe that 'I Am Who I Am'."

8.11 *Many manuscripts and early translations do not have this passage (8.1–11); others have it after Jn 21.24; others have it after Lk 21.38; one manuscript has it after Jn 7.36.*

25 "Who are you?" they asked him.

Jesus answered, "What I have told you from the very beginning.* 26 I have much to say about you, much to condemn you for. The one who sent me, however, is truthful, and I tell the world only what I have heard from him."

27 They did not understand that Jesus was talking to them about the Father. 28 So he said to them, "When you lift up the Son of Man, you will know that 'I Am Who I Am'; then you will know that I do nothing on my own authority, but I say only what the Father has instructed me to say. 29 And he who sent me is with me; he has not left me alone, because I always do what pleases him."

30 Many who heard Jesus say these things believed in him.

The Truth will Set you Free

31 So Jesus said to those who believed in him, "If you obey my teaching, you are really my disciples; 32 you will know the truth, and the truth will set you free."

33 "We are the descendants of Abraham," they answered, "and we have never been anybody's slaves. What do you mean, then, by saying, 'You will be free'?"

34 Jesus said to them, "I am telling you the truth: everyone who sins is a slave of sin. 35 A slave does not belong to a family permanently, but a son belongs there for ever. 36 If the Son sets you free, then you will be really free. 37 I know you are Abraham's descendants. Yet you are trying to kill me, because you will not accept my teaching. 38 I talk about what my Father has shown me, but you do what your father has told you."

39 They answered him, "Our father is Abraham."

"If you really were Abraham's children," Jesus replied, "you would do* the same things that he did. 40 All I have ever done is to tell you the truth I heard from God, yet you are trying to kill me. Abraham did nothing like this! 41 You are doing what your father did."

"God himself is the only Father we have," they answered, "and we are his true children."

8.25 What I have told you from the very beginning; *or* Why should I speak to you at all?
8.39 If you really were… you would do; *some manuscripts have* If you are… do.

⁴² Jesus said to them, "If God really were your Father, you would love me, because I came from God and now I am here. I did not come on my own authority, but he sent me. ⁴³ Why do you not understand what I say? It is because you cannot bear to listen to my message. ⁴⁴ You are the children of your father, the Devil, and you want to follow your father's desires. From the very beginning he was a murderer and has never been on the side of truth, because there is no truth in him. When he tells a lie, he is only doing what is natural to him, because he is a liar and the father of all lies. ⁴⁵ But I tell the truth, and that is why you do not believe me. ⁴⁶ Which one of you can prove that I am guilty of sin? If I tell the truth, then why do you not believe me? ⁴⁷ He who comes from God listens to God's words. You, however, are not from God, and that is why you will not listen."

Jesus and Abraham

⁴⁸ They asked Jesus, "Were we not right in saying that you are a Samaritan and have a demon in you?"

⁴⁹ "I have no demon," Jesus answered. "I honour my Father, but you dishonour me. ⁵⁰ I am not seeking honour for myself. But there is one who is seeking it and who judges in my favour. ⁵¹ I am telling you the truth: whoever obeys my teaching will never die."

⁵² They said to him, "Now we are certain that you have a demon! Abraham died, and the prophets died, yet you say that whoever obeys your teaching will never die. ⁵³ Our father Abraham died; you do not claim to be greater than Abraham, do you? And the prophets also died. Who do you think you are?"

⁵⁴ Jesus answered, "If I were to honour myself, that honour would be worth nothing. The one who honours me is my Father — the very one you say is your God. ⁵⁵ You have never known him, but I know him. If I were to say that I do not know him, I would be a liar like you. But I do know him, and I obey his word. ⁵⁶ Your father Abraham rejoiced that he was to see the time of my coming; he saw it and was glad."

⁵⁷ They said to him, "You are not even fifty years old — and you have seen Abraham?"*

8.57 you have seen Abraham?; *some manuscripts have* has Abraham seen you?

58 "I am telling you the truth," Jesus replied. "Before Abraham was born, 'I Am'."

59 Then they picked up stones to throw at him, but Jesus hid himself and left the Temple.

Jesus Heals a Man Born Blind

9 As Jesus was walking along, he saw a man who had been born blind. 2 His disciples asked him, "Teacher, whose sin caused him to be born blind? Was it his own or his parents' sin?"

3 Jesus answered, "His blindness has nothing to do with his sins or his parents' sins. He is blind so that God's power might be seen at work in him. 4 As long as it is day, we must keep on doing the work of him who sent me; night is coming when no one can work. 5 While I am in the world, I am the light for the world."

6 After he said this, Jesus spat on the ground and made some mud with the spittle; he rubbed the mud on the man's eyes 7 and said, "Go and wash your face in the Pool of Siloam." (This name means "Sent".) So the man went, washed his face, and came back seeing.

8 His neighbours, then, and the people who had seen him begging before this, asked, "Isn't this the man who used to sit and beg?"

9 Some said, "He is the one," but others said, "No he isn't; he just looks like him."

So the man himself said, "I am the man."

10 "How is it that you can now see?" they asked him.

11 He answered, "The man called Jesus made some mud, rubbed it on my eyes, and told me to go to Siloam and wash my face. So I went, and as soon as I washed, I could see."

12 "Where is he?" they asked.

"I don't know," he answered.

The Pharisees Investigate the Healing

13 Then they took to the Pharisees the man who had been blind. 14 The day that Jesus made the mud and cured him of his blindness was a Sabbath. 15 The Pharisees, then, asked the man again how he had received his sight. He told them, "He put some mud on my eyes; I washed my face, and now I can see."

16 Some of the Pharisees said, "The man who did this cannot be from God, for he does not obey the Sabbath law."

Others, however, said, "How could a man who is a sinner perform such miracles as these?" And there was a division among them.

17 So the Pharisees asked the man once more, "You say he cured you of your blindness — well, what do you say about him?"

"He is a prophet," the man answered.

18 The Jewish authorities, however, were not willing to believe that he had been blind and could now see, until they called his parents 19 and asked them, "Is this your son? You say that he was born blind; how is it, then, that he can now see?"

20 His parents answered, "We know that he is our son, and we know that he was born blind. 21 But we do not know how it is that he is now able to see, nor do we know who cured him of his blindness. Ask him; he is old enough, and he can answer for himself!"

22 His parents said this because they were afraid of the Jewish authorities, who had already agreed that anyone who said he believed that Jesus was the Messiah would be expelled from the synagogue. 23 That is why his parents said, "He is old enough; ask him!"

24 A second time they called back the man who had been born blind, and said to him, "Promise before God that you will tell the truth! We know that this man who cured you is a sinner."

25 "I do not know if he is a sinner or not," the man replied. "One thing I do know: I was blind, and now I see."

26 "What did he do to you?" they asked. "How did he cure you of your blindness?"

27 "I have already told you," he answered, "and you would not listen. Why do you want to hear it again? Maybe you, too, would like to be his disciples?"

28 They cursed him and said, "You are that fellow's disciple; but we are Moses' disciples. 29 We know that God spoke to Moses; as for that fellow, however, we do not even know where he comes from!"

30 The man answered, "What a strange thing that is! You do not know where he comes from, but he cured me of my blindness! 31 We know that God does not listen to sinners; he does listen to people who respect him and do what he wants them to do. 32 Since the beginning of the world nobody has ever heard of anyone giving sight to a person born blind. 33 Unless this man came from God, he would not be able to do a thing."

34 They answered, "You were born and brought up in sin — and you are trying to teach us?" And they expelled him from the synagogue.

Spiritual Blindness

35 When Jesus heard what had happened, he found the man and asked him, "Do you believe in the Son of Man?"

36 The man answered, "Tell me who he is, sir, so that I can believe in him!"

37 Jesus said to him, "You have already seen him, and he is the one who is talking with you now."

38 "I believe, Lord!" the man said, and knelt down before Jesus.

39 Jesus said, "I came to this world to judge, so that the blind should see and those who see should become blind."

40 Some Pharisees who were there with him heard him say this and asked him, "Surely you don't mean that we are blind, too?"

41 Jesus answered, "If you were blind, then you would not be guilty; but since you claim that you can see, this means that you are still guilty."

The Parable of the Shepherd

10 Jesus said, "I am telling you the truth: the man who does not enter the sheepfold by the gate, but climbs in some other way, is a thief and a robber. 2 The man who goes in through the gate is the shepherd of the sheep. 3 The gatekeeper opens the gate for him; the sheep hear his voice as he calls his own sheep by name, and he leads them out. 4 When he has brought them out, he goes ahead of them, and the sheep follow him, because they know his voice. 5 They will not follow someone else; instead, they will run away from such a person, because they do not know his voice."

6 Jesus told them this parable, but they did not understand what he meant.

Jesus the Good Shepherd

7 So Jesus said again, "I am telling you the truth: I am the gate for the sheep. 8 All others who came before me are thieves and robbers, but the sheep did not listen to them. 9 I am the gate. Whoever comes in by me will be saved; they will come in and go

out and find pasture. ¹⁰ The thief comes only in order to steal, kill, and destroy. I have come in order that you might have life — life in all its fullness.

¹¹ "I am the good shepherd, who is willing to die for the sheep. ¹² When the hired man, who is not a shepherd and does not own the sheep, sees a wolf coming, he leaves the sheep and runs away; so the wolf snatches the sheep and scatters them. ¹³ The hired man runs away because he is only a hired man and does not care about the sheep. ¹⁴⁻¹⁵ I am the good shepherd. As the Father knows me and I know the Father, in the same way I know my sheep and they know me. And I am willing to die for them. ¹⁶ There are other sheep which belong to me that are not in this sheepfold. I must bring them, too; they will listen to my voice, and they will become* one flock with one shepherd.

¹⁷ "The Father loves me because I am willing to give up my life, in order that I may receive it back again. ¹⁸ No one takes my life away from me. I give it up of my own free will. I have the right to give it up, and I have the right to take it back. This is what my Father has commanded me to do."

¹⁹ Again there was a division among the people because of these words. ²⁰ Many of them were saying, "He has a demon! He is mad! Why do you listen to him?"

²¹ But others were saying, "A man with a demon could not talk like this! How could a demon give sight to blind people?"

Jesus is Rejected

²² It was winter, and the Festival of the Dedication of the Temple was being celebrated in Jerusalem. ²³ Jesus was walking in Solomon's Porch in the Temple, ²⁴ when the people gathered round him and asked, "How long are you going to keep us in suspense? Tell us the plain truth: are you the Messiah?"

²⁵ Jesus answered, "I have already told you, but you would not believe me. The things I do by my Father's authority speak on my behalf; ²⁶ but you will not believe, for you are not my sheep. ²⁷ My sheep listen to my voice; I know them, and they follow me. ²⁸ I give them eternal life, and they shall never die. No one can snatch them away from me. ²⁹ What my Father has given

---

10.16 they will become; *some manuscripts have* there will be.

me is greater* than everything, and no one can snatch them away from the Father's care. 30 The Father and I are one."

31 Then the people again picked up stones to throw at him. 32 Jesus said to them, "I have done many good deeds in your presence which the Father gave me to do; for which one of these do you want to stone me?"

33 They replied, "We do not want to stone you because of any good deeds, but because of your blasphemy! You are only a man, but you are trying to make yourself God!"

34 Jesus answered, "It is written in your own Law that God said, 'You are gods.' 35 We know that what the scripture says is true for ever; and God called those people gods, the people to whom his message was given. 36 As for me, the Father chose me and sent me into the world. How, then, can you say that I blaspheme because I said that I am the Son of God? 37 Do not believe me, then, if I am not doing the things my Father wants me to do. 38 But if I do them, even though you do not believe me, you should at least believe my deeds, in order that you may know once and for all that the Father is in me and that I am in the Father."

39 Once more they tried to seize Jesus, but he slipped out of their hands.

40 Jesus then went back again across the River Jordan to the place where John had been baptizing, and he stayed there. 41 Many people came to him. "John performed no miracles," they said, "but everything he said about this man was true." 42 And many people there believed in him.

The Death of Lazarus

11 A man named Lazarus, who lived in Bethany, was ill. Bethany was the town where Mary and her sister Martha lived. 2 (This Mary was the one who poured the perfume on the Lord's feet and wiped them with her hair; it was her brother Lazarus who was ill.) 3 The sisters sent Jesus a message: "Lord, your dear friend is ill."

4 When Jesus heard it, he said, "The final result of this illness will not be the death of Lazarus; this has happened in order to

---

10.29 What my Father has given me is greater; *some manuscripts have* My Father, who gave them to me, is greater.

bring glory to God, and it will be the means by which the Son of God will receive glory."

5 Jesus loved Martha and her sister and Lazarus. 6 Yet when he received the news that Lazarus was ill, he stayed where he was for two more days. 7 Then he said to the disciples, "Let us go back to Judea."

8 "Teacher," the disciples answered, "just a short time ago the people there wanted to stone you; and are you planning to go back?"

9 Jesus said, "A day has twelve hours, hasn't it? So whoever walks in broad daylight does not stumble, for they see the light of this world. 10 But if they walk during the night they stumble, because they have no light." 11 Jesus said this and then added, "Our friend Lazarus has fallen asleep, but I will go and wake him up."

12 The disciples answered, "If he is asleep, Lord, he will get well."

13 Jesus meant that Lazarus had died, but they thought he meant natural sleep. 14 So Jesus told them plainly, "Lazarus is dead, 15 but for your sake I am glad that I was not with him, so that you will believe. Let us go to him."

16 Thomas (called the Twin) said to his fellow-disciples, "Let us all go with the Teacher, so that we may die with him!"

Jesus the Resurrection and the Life

17 When Jesus arrived, he found that Lazarus had been buried four days before. 18 Bethany was less than three kilometres from Jerusalem, 19 and many Judeans had come to see Martha and Mary to comfort them over their brother's death.

20 When Martha heard that Jesus was coming, she went out to meet him, but Mary stayed in the house. 21 Martha said to Jesus, "If you had been here, Lord, my brother would not have died! 22 But I know that even now God will give you whatever you ask him for."

23 "Your brother will rise to life," Jesus told her.

24 "I know," she replied, "that he will rise to life on the last day."

25 Jesus said to her, "I am the resurrection and the life. Those who believe in me will live, even though they die; 26 and all those who live and believe in me will never die. Do you believe this?"

27 "Yes, Lord!" she answered. "I do believe that you are the Messiah, the Son of God, who was to come into the world."

Jesus Weeps

28 After Martha said this, she went back and called her sister Mary privately. "The Teacher is here," she told her, "and is asking for you." 29 When Mary heard this, she got up and hurried out to meet him. 30 (Jesus had not yet arrived in the village, but was still in the place where Martha had met him.) 31 The people who were in the house with Mary, comforting her, followed her when they saw her get up and hurry out. They thought that she was going to the grave to weep there.

32 Mary arrived where Jesus was, and as soon as she saw him, she fell at his feet. "Lord," she said, "if you had been here, my brother would not have died!"

33 Jesus saw her weeping, and he saw how the people who were with her were weeping also; his heart was touched, and he was deeply moved. 34 "Where have you buried him?" he asked them.

"Come and see, Lord," they answered.

35 Jesus wept. 36 "See how much he loved him!" the people said.

37 But some of them said, "He gave sight to the blind man, didn't he? Could he not have kept Lazarus from dying?"

Lazarus is Brought to Life

38 Deeply moved once more, Jesus went to the tomb, which was a cave with a stone placed at the entrance. 39 "Take the stone away!" Jesus ordered.

Martha, the dead man's sister, answered, "There will be a bad smell, Lord. He has been buried four days!"

Lazarus, come out!   (11.43)

40 Jesus said to her, "Didn't I tell you that you would see God's glory if you believed?" 41 They took the stone away. Jesus looked up and said, "I thank you, Father, that you listen to me. 42 I know that you always listen to me, but I say this for the sake of the people here, so that they will believe that you sent me." 43 After he had said this, he called out in a loud voice, "Lazarus, come out!" 44 He came out, his hands and feet wrapped in grave clothes, and with a cloth round his face. "Untie him," Jesus told them, "and let him go."

The Plot against Jesus
(Mt 26.1–5; Mk 14.1–2; Lk 22.1–2)

45 Many of the people who had come to visit Mary saw what Jesus did, and they believed in him. 46 But some of them returned to the Pharisees and told them what Jesus had done. 47 So the Pharisees and the chief priests met with the Council and said, "What shall we do? Look at all the miracles this man is performing! 48 If we let him go on in this way, everyone will believe in him, and the Roman authorities will take action and destroy our Temple and our nation!"

49 One of them, named Caiaphas, who was High Priest that year, said, "What fools you are! 50 Don't you realize that it is better for you to let one man die for the people, instead of having the whole nation destroyed?" 51 Actually, he did not say this of his own accord; rather, as he was High Priest that year, he was prophesying that Jesus was going to die for the Jewish people, 52 and not only for them, but also to bring together into one body all the scattered people of God.

53 From that day on the Jewish authorities made plans to kill Jesus. 54 So Jesus did not travel openly in Judea, but left and went to a place near the desert, to a town named Ephraim, where he stayed with the disciples.

55 The time for the Passover Festival was near, and many people went up from the country to Jerusalem to perform the ritual of purification before the festival. 56 They were looking for Jesus, and as they gathered in the Temple, they asked one another, "What do you think? Surely he will not come to the festival, will he?" 57 The chief priests and the Pharisees had given orders that if anyone knew where Jesus was, he must report it, so that they could arrest him.

Jesus is Anointed at Bethany
(Mt 26.6–13; Mk 14.3–9)

12 Six days before the Passover, Jesus went to Bethany, the home of Lazarus, the man he had raised from death. 2 They prepared a dinner for him there, which Martha helped to serve; Lazarus was one of those who were sitting at the table with Jesus. 3 Then Mary took half a litre of a very expensive perfume made of pure nard, poured it on Jesus' feet, and wiped them with her hair. The sweet smell of the perfume filled the whole house. 4 One of Jesus' disciples, Judas Iscariot — the one who was going to betray him — said, 5 "Why wasn't this perfume sold for three hundred silver coins* and the money given to the poor?" 6 He said this, not because he cared about the poor, but because he was a thief. He carried the money bag and would help himself from it.

7 But Jesus said, "Leave her alone! Let her keep what she has for the day of my burial. 8 You will always have poor people with you, but you will not always have me."

The Plot against Lazarus

9 A large number of people heard that Jesus was in Bethany, so they went there, not only because of Jesus but also to see Lazarus, whom Jesus had raised from death. 10 So the chief priests made plans to kill Lazarus too, 11 because on his account many Jews were rejecting them and believing in Jesus.

The Triumphant Entry into Jerusalem
(Mt 21.1–11; Mk 11.1–11; Lk 19.28–40)

12 The next day the large crowd that had come to the Passover Festival heard that Jesus was coming to Jerusalem. 13 So they took branches of palm trees and went out to meet him, shouting, "Praise God! God bless him who comes in the name of the Lord! God bless the King of Israel!"

14 Jesus found a donkey and rode on it, just as the scripture says,
15 "Do not be afraid, city of Zion!
    Here comes your king,
        riding on a young donkey."

12.5 SILVER COINS: *See 6.7.*

16 His disciples did not understand this at the time; but when Jesus had been raised to glory, they remembered that the scripture said this about him and that they had done this for him.

17 The people who had been with Jesus when he called Lazarus out of the grave and raised him from death had reported what had happened. 18 That was why the crowd met him — because they heard that he had performed this miracle. 19 The Pharisees then said to one another, "You see, we are not succeeding at all! Look, the whole world is following him!"

Some Greeks Seek Jesus

20 Some Greeks were among those who had gone to Jerusalem to worship during the festival. 21 They went to Philip (he was from Bethsaida in Galilee) and said, "Sir, we want to see Jesus."

22 Philip went and told Andrew, and the two of them went and told Jesus. 23 Jesus answered them, "The hour has now come for the Son of Man to receive great glory. 24 I am telling you the truth: a grain of wheat remains no more than a single grain unless it is dropped into the ground and dies. If it does die, then it produces many grains. 25 Those who love their own life will lose it; those who hate their own life in this world will keep it for life eternal. 26 Whoever wants to serve me must follow me, so that my servant will be with me where I am. And my Father will honour anyone who serves me.

Jesus Speaks about his Death

27 "Now my heart is troubled — and what shall I say? Shall I say, 'Father, do not let this hour come upon me'? But that is why I came — so that I might go through this hour of suffering. 28 Father, bring glory to your name!"

Then a voice spoke from heaven, "I have brought glory to it, and I will do so again."

29 The crowd standing there heard the voice, and some of them said it was thunder, while others said, "An angel spoke to him!"

30 But Jesus said to them, "It was not for my sake that this voice spoke, but for yours. 31 Now is the time for this world to be judged; now the ruler of this world will be overthrown. 32 When I am lifted up from the earth, I will draw everyone to me." 33 (In saying this he indicated the kind of death he was going to suffer.)

34 The crowd answered, "Our Law tells us that the Messiah will live for ever. How, then, can you say that the Son of Man must be lifted up? Who is this Son of Man?"

35 Jesus answered, "The light will be among you a little longer. Continue on your way while you have the light, so that the darkness will not come upon you; for the one who walks in the dark does not know where he is going. 36 Believe in the light, then, while you have it, so that you will be the people of the light."

The Unbelief of the People

After Jesus said this, he went off and hid himself from them. 37 Even though he had performed all these miracles in their presence, they did not believe in him, 38 so that what the prophet Isaiah had said might come true:

"Lord, who believed the message we told?
To whom did the Lord reveal his power?"

39 And so they were not able to believe, because Isaiah also said:

40 "God has blinded their eyes
and closed their minds,
so that their eyes would not see,
and their minds would not understand,
and they would not turn to me, says God,
for me to heal them."

41 Isaiah said this because he saw Jesus' glory and spoke about him.

42 Even then, many of the Jewish authorities believed in Jesus; but because of the Pharisees they did not talk about it openly, so as not to be expelled from the synagogue. 43 They loved human approval rather than the approval of God.

Judgement by Jesus' Words

44 Jesus said in a loud voice, "Whoever believes in me believes not only in me but also in him who sent me. 45 Whoever sees me sees also him who sent me. 46 I have come into the world as light, so that everyone who believes in me should not remain in the darkness. 47 If anyone hears my message and does not obey it, I will not judge him. I came, not to judge the world, but to save it. 48 Those who reject me and do not accept my message have one

who will judge them. The words I have spoken will be their judge on the last day! 49 This is true, because I have not spoken on my own authority, but the Father who sent me has commanded me what I must say and speak. 50 And I know that his command brings eternal life. What I say, then, is what the Father has told me to say."

Jesus Washes his Disciples' Feet

13 It was now the day before the Passover Festival. Jesus knew that the hour had come for him to leave this world and go to the Father. He had always loved those in the world who were his own, and he loved them to the very end.

2 Jesus and his disciples were at supper. The Devil had already put into the heart of Judas, the son of Simon Iscariot, the thought of betraying Jesus.* 3 Jesus knew that the Father had given him complete power; he knew that he had come from God and was going to God. 4 So he rose from the table, took off his outer garment, and tied a towel round his waist. 5 Then he poured some water into a basin and began to wash the disciples' feet and dry them with the towel round his waist. 6 He came to Simon Peter, who said to him, "Are you going to wash my feet, Lord?"

7 Jesus answered him, "You do not understand now what I am doing, but you will understand later."

8 Peter declared, "Never at any time will you wash my feet!"

"If I do not wash your feet," Jesus answered, "you will no longer be my disciple."

9 Simon Peter answered, "Lord, do not wash only my feet, then! Wash my hands and head, too!"

10 Jesus said, "Those who have had a bath are completely clean and do not have to wash themselves, except for their feet.* All of you are clean — all except one." 11 (Jesus already knew who was going to betray him; that is why he said, "All of you, except one, are clean.")

12 After Jesus had washed their feet, he put his outer garment back on and returned to his place at the table. "Do you understand

---

13.2 The Devil… betraying Jesus; *or* The Devil had already decided that Judas, the son of Simon Iscariot, would betray Jesus.
13.10 *Some manuscripts do not have* except for their feet.

what I have just done to you?" he asked. 13 "You call me Teacher and Lord, and it is right that you do so, because that is what I am. 14 I, your Lord and Teacher, have just washed your feet. You, then, should wash one another's feet. 15 I have set an example for you, so that you will do just what I have done for you. 16 I am telling you the truth: slaves are never greater than their master, and messengers are never greater than the one who sent them. 17 Now that you know this truth, how happy you will be if you put it into practice!

18 "I am not talking about all of you; I know those I have chosen. But the scripture must come true that says, 'The man who shared my food turned against me.' 19 I tell you this now before it happens, so that when it does happen, you will believe that 'I Am Who I Am.' 20 I am telling you the truth: whoever receives anyone I send receives me also; and whoever receives me receives him who sent me."

Jesus Predicts his Betrayal
(Mt 26.20–25; Mk 14.17–21; Lk 22.21–23)

21 After Jesus had said this, he was deeply troubled and declared openly, "I am telling you the truth: one of you is going to betray me."

22 The disciples looked at one another, completely puzzled about whom he meant. 23 One of the disciples, the one whom Jesus loved, was sitting next to Jesus. 24 Simon Peter motioned to him and said, "Ask him whom he is talking about."

The disciples looked at one another   (13.22)

25 So that disciple moved closer to Jesus' side and asked, "Who is it, Lord?"

26 Jesus answered, "I will dip some bread in the sauce and give it to him; he is the man." So he took a piece of bread, dipped it, and gave it to Judas, the son of Simon Iscariot. 27 As soon as Judas took the bread, Satan entered him. Jesus said to him, "Be quick about

what you are doing!" ²⁸ None of the others at the table under-stood why Jesus said this to him. ²⁹ Since Judas was in charge of the money bag, some of the disciples thought that Jesus had told him to go and buy what they needed for the festival, or to give something to the poor.

³⁰ Judas accepted the bread and went out at once. It was night.

The New Commandment

³¹ After Judas had left, Jesus said, "Now the Son of Man's glory is revealed; now God's glory is revealed through him. ³² And if God's glory is revealed through him, then God will reveal the glory of the Son of Man in himself, and he will do so at once. ³³ My children, I shall not be with you very much longer. You will look for me; but I tell you now what I told the Jewish authorities, 'You cannot go where I am going.' ³⁴ And now I give you a new commandment: love one another. As I have loved you, so you must love one another. ³⁵ If you have love for one another, then everyone will know that you are my disciples."

Jesus Predicts Peter's Denial
(Mt 26.31–35; Mk 14.27–31; Lk 22.31–34)

³⁶ "Where are you going, Lord?" Simon Peter asked him.

"You cannot follow me now where I am going," answered Jesus; "but later you will follow me."

³⁷ "Lord, why can't I follow you now?" asked Peter. "I am ready to die for you!"

³⁸ Jesus answered, "Are you really ready to die for me? I am telling you the truth: before the cock crows you will say three times that you do not know me.

Jesus the Way to the Father

14 "Do not be worried and upset," Jesus told them. "Believe* in God and believe also in me. ² There are many rooms in my Father's house, and I am going to prepare a place for you. I would not tell you this if it were not so.* ³ And after I go and

---

14.1 Believe; *or* You believe.
14.2 There are… were not so; *or* There are many rooms in my Father's house; if it were not so, would I tell you that I am going to prepare a place for you?

prepare a place for you, I will come back and take you to myself, so that you will be where I am. 4 You know the way that leads to the place where I am going."

5 Thomas said to him, "Lord, we do not know where you are going; so how can we know the way to get there?"

6 Jesus answered him, "I am the way, the truth, and the life; no one goes to the Father except by me. 7 Now that you have known me," he said to them, "you will know* my Father also, and from now on you do know him and you have seen him."

8 Philip said to him, "Lord, show us the Father; that is all we need."

9 Jesus answered, "For a long time I have been with you all; yet you do not know me, Philip? Whoever has seen me has seen the Father. Why, then, do you say, 'Show us the Father'? 10 Do you not believe, Philip, that I am in the Father and the Father is in me? The words that I have spoken to you," Jesus said to his disciples, "do not come from me. The Father, who remains in me, does his own work. 11 Believe me when I say that I am in the Father and the Father is in me. If not, believe because of the things I do. 12 I am telling you the truth: those who believe in me will do what I do — yes, they will do even greater things, because I am going to the Father. 13 And I will do whatever you ask for in my name, so that the Father's glory will be shown through the Son. 14 If you ask me* for anything in my name, I will do it.

The Promise of the Holy Spirit

15 "If you love me, you will obey my commandments. 16 I will ask the Father, and he will give you another Helper, who will stay with you for ever. 17 He is the Spirit who reveals the truth about God. The world cannot receive him, because it cannot see him or know him. But you know him, because he remains with you and is* in you.

18 "When I go, you will not be left all alone; I will come back to you. 19 In a little while the world will see me no more, but you will see me; and because I live, you also will live. 20 When that day

---

14.7 Now that you have known me... you will know; *some manuscripts have* If you had known me... you would know.
14.14 *Some manuscripts do not have* me.
14.17 is; *some manuscripts have* will be.

comes, you will know that I am in my Father and that you are in me, just as I am in you.

21 "Those who accept my commandments and obey them are the ones who love me. My Father will love those who love me; I too will love them and reveal myself to them."

22 Judas (not Judas Iscariot) said, "Lord, how can it be that you will reveal yourself to us and not to the world?"

23 Jesus answered him, "Whoever loves me will obey my teaching. My Father will love him, and my Father and I will come to him and live with him. 24 Whoever does not love me does not obey my teaching. And the teaching you have heard is not mine, but comes from the Father, who sent me.

25 "I have told you this while I am still with you. 26 The Helper, the Holy Spirit, whom the Father will send in my name, will teach you everything and make you remember all that I have told you.

27 "Peace is what I leave with you; it is my own peace that I give you. I do not give it as the world does. Do not be worried and upset; do not be afraid. 28 You heard me say to you, 'I am leaving, but I will come back to you.' If you loved me, you would be glad that I am going to the Father; for he is greater than I. 29 I have told you this now before it all happens, so that when it does happen, you will believe. 30 I cannot talk with you much longer, because the ruler of this world is coming. He has no power over me, 31 but the world must know that I love the Father; that is why I do everything as he commands me.

"Come, let us go from this place.

Jesus the Real Vine

15 "I am the real vine, and my Father is the gardener. 2 He breaks off every branch in me that does not bear fruit, and he prunes every branch that does bear fruit, so that it will be clean and bear more fruit. 3 You have been made clean already by the teaching I have given you. 4 Remain united to me, and I will remain united to you. A branch cannot bear fruit by itself; it can do so only if it remains in the vine. In the same way you cannot bear fruit unless you remain in me.

5 "I am the vine, and you are the branches. Those who remain in me, and I in them, will bear much fruit; for you can do nothing without me. 6 Whoever does not remain in me is thrown out like

a branch and dries up; such branches are gathered up and thrown into the fire, where they are burnt. 7 If you remain in me and my words remain in you, then you will ask for anything you wish, and you shall have it. 8 My Father's glory is shown by your bearing much fruit; and in this way you become my disciples. 9 I love you just as the Father loves me; remain in my love. 10 If you obey my commands, you will remain in my love, just as I have obeyed my Father's commands and remain in his love.

11 "I have told you this so that my joy may be in you and that your joy may be complete. 12 My commandment is this: love one another, just as I love you. 13 The greatest love a person can have for his friends is to give his life for them. 14 And you are my friends if you do what I command you. 15 I do not call you servants any longer, because servants do not know what their master is doing. Instead, I call you friends, because I have told you everything I have heard from my Father. 16 You did not choose me; I chose you and appointed you to go and bear much fruit, the kind of fruit that endures. And so the Father will give you whatever you ask of him in my name. 17 This, then, is what I command you: love one another.

The World's Hatred

18 "If the world hates you, just remember that it has hated me first. 19 If you belonged to the world, then the world would love you as its own. But I chose you from this world, and you do not belong to it; that is why the world hates you. 20 Remember what I told you: 'Slaves are not greater than their master.' If people persecuted me, they will persecute you too; if they obeyed my teaching, they will obey yours too. 21 But they will do all this to you because you are mine; for they do not know the one who sent me. 22 They would not have been guilty of sin if I had not come and spoken to them; as it is, they no longer have any excuse for their sin. 23 Whoever hates me hates my Father also. 24 They would not have been guilty of sin if I had not done among them the things that no one else ever did; as it is, they have seen what I did, and they hate both me and my Father. 25 This, however, was bound to happen so that what is written in their Law may come true: 'They hated me for no reason at all.'

26 "The Helper will come — the Spirit, who reveals the truth about God and who comes from the Father. I will send him to you

from the Father, and he will speak about me. 27 And you, too, will speak about me, because you have been with me from the very beginning.

16 "I have told you this, so that you will not give up your faith. 2 You will be expelled from the synagogues, and the time will come when anyone who kills you will think that by doing this he is serving God. 3 People will do these things to you because they have not known either the Father or me. 4 But I have told you this, so that when the time comes for them to do these things, you will remember that I told you.

The Work of the Holy Spirit

"I did not tell you these things at the beginning, for I was with you. 5 But now I am going to him who sent me, yet none of you asks me where I am going. 6 And now that I have told you, your hearts are full of sadness. 7 But I am telling you the truth: it is better for you that I go away, because if I do not go, the Helper will not come to you. But if I do go away, then I will send him to you. 8 And when he comes, he will prove to the people of the world that they are wrong about sin and about what is right and about God's judgement. 9 They are wrong about sin, because they do not believe in me; 10 they are wrong about what is right, because I am going to the Father and you will not see me any more; 11 and they are wrong about judgement, because the ruler of this world has already been judged.

12 "I have much more to tell you, but now it would be too much for you to bear. 13 When, however, the Spirit comes, who reveals the truth about God, he will lead you into all the truth. He will not speak on his own authority, but he will speak of what he hears, and will tell you of things to come. 14 He will give me glory, because he will take what I say and tell it to you. 15 All that my Father has is mine; that is why I said that the Spirit will take what I give him and tell it to you.

Sadness and Gladness

16 "In a little while you will not see me any more, and then a little while later you will see me."

17 Some of his disciples asked among themselves, "What does this mean? He tells us that in a little while we will not see him,

and then a little while later we will see him; and he also says, 'It is because I am going to the Father.' 18 What does this 'a little while' mean? We don't know what he is talking about!"

19 Jesus knew that they wanted to question him, so he said to them, "I said, 'In a little while you will not see me, and then a little while later you will see me.' Is this what you are asking about among yourselves? 20 I am telling you the truth: you will cry and weep, but the world will be glad; you will be sad, but your sadness will turn into gladness. 21 When a woman is about to give birth, she is sad because her hour of suffering has come; but when the baby is born, she forgets her suffering, because she is happy that a baby has been born into the world. 22 That is how it is with you: now you are sad, but I will see you again, and your hearts will be filled with gladness, the kind of gladness that no one can take away from you.

23 "When that day comes, you will not ask me for anything. I am telling you the truth: the Father will give you whatever you ask him for in my name.* 24 Until now you have not asked for anything in my name; ask and you will receive, so that your happiness may be complete.

Victory over the World

25 "I have used figures of speech to tell you these things. But the time will come when I will not use figures of speech, but will speak to you plainly about the Father. 26 When that day comes, you will ask him in my name; and I do not say that I will ask him on your behalf, 27 for the Father himself loves you. He loves you because you love me and have believed that I came from God. 28 I did come from the Father, and I came into the world; and now I am leaving the world and going to the Father."

29 Then his disciples said to him, "Now you are speaking plainly, without using figures of speech. 30 We know now that you know everything; you do not need someone to ask you questions. This makes us believe that you came from God."

31 Jesus answered them, "Do you believe now? 32 The time is coming, and is already here, when all of you will be scattered,

---

16.23 the Father will give you whatever you ask him for in my name; *some manuscripts have* if you ask the Father for anything, he will give it to you in my name.

each of you to your own home, and I will be left all alone. But I am not really alone, because the Father is with me. 33 I have told you this so that you will have peace by being united to me. The world will make you suffer. But be brave! I have defeated the world!"

Jesus Prays for his Disciples

17 After Jesus finished saying this, he looked up to heaven and said, "Father, the hour has come. Give glory to your Son, so that the Son may give glory to you. 2 For you gave him authority over all humanity, so that he might give eternal life to all those you gave him. 3 And eternal life means knowing you, the only true God, and knowing Jesus Christ, whom you sent. 4 I have shown your glory on earth; I have finished the work you gave me to do. 5 Father! Give me glory in your presence now, the same glory I had with you before the world was made.

Father, the hour has come   (17.1)

6 "I have made you known to those you gave me out of the world. They belonged to you, and you gave them to me. They have obeyed your word, 7 and now they know that everything you gave me comes from you. 8 I gave them the message that you gave me, and they received it; they know that it is true that I came from you, and they believe that you sent me.

9 "I pray for them. I do not pray for the world but for those you gave me, for they belong to you. 10 All I have is yours, and all you have is mine; and my glory is shown through them. 11 And now I

am coming to you; I am no longer in the world, but they are in the world. Holy Father! Keep them safe by the power of your name, the name you gave me,* so that they may be one just as you and I are one. 12 While I was with them, I kept them safe by the power of your name, the name you gave me.* I protected them, and not one of them was lost, except the man who was bound to be lost — so that the scripture might come true. 13 And now I am coming to you, and I say these things in the world so that they might have my joy in their hearts in all its fullness. 14 I gave them your message, and the world hated them, because they do not belong to the world, just as I do not belong to the world. 15 I do not ask you to take them out of the world, but I do ask you to keep them safe from the Evil One. 16 Just as I do not belong to the world, they do not belong to the world. 17 Dedicate them to yourself by means of the truth; your word is truth. 18 I sent them into the world, just as you sent me into the world. 19 And for their sake I dedicate myself to you, in order that they, too, may be truly dedicated to you.

20 "I pray not only for them, but also for those who believe in me because of their message. 21 I pray that they may all be one. Father! May they be in us, just as you are in me and I am in you. May they be one, so that the world will believe that you sent me. 22 I gave them the same glory you gave me, so that they may be one, just as you and I are one: 23 I in them and you in me, so that they may be completely one, in order that the world may know that you sent me and that you love them as you love me.

24 "Father! You have given them to me, and I want them to be with me where I am, so that they may see my glory, the glory you gave me; for you loved me before the world was made. 25 Righteous Father! The world does not know you, but I know you, and these know that you sent me. 26 I made you known to them, and I will continue to do so, in order that the love you have for me may be in them, and so that I also may be in them."

17.11 Keep them safe by the power of your name, the name you gave me; *some manuscripts have* By the power of your name keep safe those you have given me.

17.12 I kept them safe by the power of your name, the name you gave me; *some manuscripts have* By the power of your name I kept safe those you have given me.

The Arrest of Jesus

(Mt 26.47–56; Mk 14.43–50; Lk 22.47–53)

18 After Jesus had said this prayer, he left with his disciples and went across the brook called Kidron. There was a garden in that place, and Jesus and his disciples went in. 2 Judas, the traitor, knew where it was, because many times Jesus had met there with his disciples. 3 So Judas went to the garden, taking with him a group of Roman soldiers, and some temple guards sent by the chief priests and the Pharisees; they were armed and carried lanterns and torches. 4 Jesus knew everything that was going to happen to him, so he stepped forward and asked them, "Who is it you are looking for?"

5 "Jesus of Nazareth," they answered.

"I am he," he said.

Judas, the traitor, was standing there with them. 6 When Jesus said to them, "I am he," they moved back and fell to the ground. 7 Again Jesus asked them, "Who is it you are looking for?"

"Jesus of Nazareth," they said.

8 "I have already told you that I am he," Jesus said. "If, then, you are looking for me, let these others go." 9 (He said this so that what he had said might come true: "Father, I have not lost even one of those you gave me.")

10 Simon Peter, who had a sword, drew it and struck the High Priest's slave, cutting off his right ear. The name of the slave was Malchus. 11 Jesus said to Peter, "Put your sword back in its place! Do you think that I will not drink the cup of suffering which my Father has given me?"

Jesus before Annas

12 Then the Roman soldiers with their commanding officer and the Jewish guards arrested Jesus, bound him, 13 and took him first to Annas. He was the father-in-law of Caiaphas, who was High Priest that year. 14 It was Caiaphas who had advised the Jewish authorities that it was better that one man should die for all the people.

Peter Denies Jesus

(Mt 26.69–70; Mk 14.66–68; Lk 22.55–57)

15 Simon Peter and another disciple followed Jesus. That other disciple was well known to the High Priest, so he went with Jesus into the courtyard of the High Priest's house, 16 while Peter stayed

outside by the gate. Then the other disciple went back out, spoke to the girl at the gate, and brought Peter inside. 17 The girl at the gate said to Peter, "Aren't you also one of the disciples of that man?"

"No, I am not," answered Peter.

18 It was cold, so the servants and guards had built a charcoal fire and were standing round it, warming themselves. So Peter went over and stood with them, warming himself.

The High Priest Questions Jesus
(Mt 26.59–66; Mk 14.55–64; Lk 22.66–71)

19 The High Priest questioned Jesus about his disciples and about his teaching. 20 Jesus answered, "I have always spoken publicly to everyone; all my teaching was done in the synagogues and in the Temple, where all the people come together. I have never said anything in secret. 21 Why, then, do you question me? Question the people who heard me. Ask them what I told them — they know what I said."

22 When Jesus said this, one of the guards there slapped him and said, "How dare you talk like that to the High Priest!"

23 Jesus answered him, "If I have said anything wrong, tell everyone here what it was. But if I am right in what I have said, why do you hit me?"

24 Then Annas sent him, still bound, to Caiaphas the High Priest.

Peter Denies Jesus Again
(Mt 26.71–75; Mk 14.69–72; Lk 22.58–62)

25 Peter was still standing there keeping himself warm. So the others said to him, "Aren't you also one of the disciples of that man?"

But Peter denied it. "No, I am not," he said.

26 One of the High Priest's slaves, a relative of the man whose ear Peter had cut off, spoke up. "Didn't I see you with him in the garden?" he asked.

27 Again Peter said "No" — and at once a cock crowed.

Jesus is Brought before Pilate
(Mt 27.1–2, 11–14; Mk 15.1–5; Lk 23.1–5)

28 Early in the morning Jesus was taken from Caiaphas' house to the governor's palace. The Jewish authorities did not go inside

the palace, for they wanted to keep themselves ritually clean, in order to be able to eat the Passover meal. 29 So Pilate went outside to them and asked, "What do you accuse this man of?"

30 Their answer was, "We would not have brought him to you if he had not committed a crime."

31 Pilate said to them, "Then you yourselves take him and try him according to your own law."

They replied, "We are not allowed to put anyone to death." 32 (This happened in order to make the words of Jesus come true, the words he used when he indicated the kind of death he would die.)

33 Pilate went back into the palace and called Jesus. "Are you the King of the Jews?" he asked him.

34 Jesus answered, "Does this question come from you or have others told you about me?"

35 Pilate replied, "Do you think I am a Jew? It was your own people and the chief priests who handed you over to me. What have you done?"

36 Jesus said, "My kingdom does not belong to this world; if my kingdom belonged to this world, my followers would fight to keep me from being handed over to the Jewish authorities. No, my kingdom does not belong here!"

37 So Pilate asked him, "Are you a king, then?"

Jesus answered, "You say that I am a king. I was born and came into the world for this one purpose, to speak about the truth. Whoever belongs to the truth listens to me."

38 "And what is truth?" Pilate asked.

And what is truth?   (18.38)

Jesus is Sentenced to Death

(Mt 27.15–31; Mk 15.6–20; Lk 23.13–25)

Then Pilate went back outside to the people and said to them, "I cannot find any reason to condemn him. 39 But according to the custom you have, I always set free a prisoner for you during the Passover. Do you want me to set free for you the King of the Jews?"

40 They answered him with a shout, "No, not him! We want Barabbas!" (Barabbas was a bandit.)

No, not him! We want Barabbas!   (18.40)

19 Then Pilate took Jesus and had him whipped. 2 The soldiers made a crown out of thorny branches and put it on his head; then they put a purple robe on him 3 and came to him and said, "Long live the King of the Jews!" And they went up and slapped him.

4 Pilate went out once more and said to the crowd, "Look, I will bring him out here to you to let you see that I cannot find any reason to condemn him." 5 So Jesus came out, wearing the crown of thorns and the purple robe. Pilate said to them, "Look! Here is the man!"

6 When the chief priests and the temple guards saw him, they shouted, "Crucify him! Crucify him!"

Pilate said to them, "You take him, then, and crucify him. I find no reason to condemn him."

7 The crowd answered back, "We have a law that says he ought to die, because he claimed to be the Son of God."

⁸ When Pilate heard this, he was even more afraid. ⁹ He went back into the palace and asked Jesus, "Where do you come from?"

But Jesus did not answer. ¹⁰ Pilate said to him, "You will not speak to me? Remember, I have the authority to set you free and also to have you crucified."

¹¹ Jesus answered, "You have authority over me only because it was given to you by God. So the man who handed me over to you is guilty of a worse sin."

¹² When Pilate heard this, he tried to find a way to set Jesus free. But the crowd shouted back, "If you set him free, that means that you are not the Emperor's friend! Anyone who claims to be a king is a rebel against the Emperor!"

¹³ When Pilate heard these words, he took Jesus outside and sat down on the judge's seat in the place called "The Stone Pavement". (In Hebrew the name is "Gabbatha".) ¹⁴ It was then almost noon of the day before the Passover. Pilate said to the people, "Here is your king!"

¹⁵ They shouted back, "Kill him! Kill him! Crucify him!"

Pilate asked them, "Do you want me to crucify your king?"

The chief priests answered, "The only king we have is the Emperor!"

¹⁶ Then Pilate handed Jesus over to them to be crucified.

Jesus is Crucified
(Mt 27.32–44; Mk 15.21–32; Lk 23.26–43)

So they took charge of Jesus. ¹⁷ He went out, carrying his cross, and came to "The Place of the Skull", as it is called. (In Hebrew it is called "Golgotha".) ¹⁸ There they crucified him; and they also crucified two other men, one on each side, with Jesus between them. ¹⁹ Pilate wrote a notice and had it put on the cross. "Jesus of Nazareth, the King of the Jews", is what he wrote. ²⁰ Many people read it, because the place where Jesus was crucified was not far from the city. The notice was written in Hebrew, Latin, and Greek. ²¹ The chief priests said to Pilate, "Do not write 'The King of the Jews', but rather, 'This man said, I am the King of the Jews.' "

²² Pilate answered, "What I have written stays written."

²³ After the soldiers had crucified Jesus, they took his clothes and divided them into four parts, one part for each soldier. They also

took the robe, which was made of one piece of woven cloth without any seams in it. 24 The soldiers said to one another, "Let's not tear it; let's throw dice to see who will get it." This happened in order to make the scripture come true:

"They divided my clothes among themselves
and gambled for my robe."
And this is what the soldiers did.

25 Standing close to Jesus' cross were his mother, his mother's sister, Mary the wife of Clopas, and Mary Magdalene. 26 Jesus saw his mother and the disciple he loved standing there; so he said to his mother, "He is your son."

27 Then he said to the disciple, "She is your mother." From that time the disciple took her to live in his home.

The Death of Jesus
(Mt 27.45–56; Mk 15.33–41; Lk 23.44–49)

28 Jesus knew that by now everything had been completed; and in order to make the scripture come true, he said, "I am thirsty."

29 A bowl was there, full of cheap wine; so a sponge was soaked in the wine, put on a stalk of hyssop, and lifted up to his lips. 30 Jesus drank the wine and said, "It is finished!"

Then he bowed his head and died.

Jesus' Side is Pierced

31 Then the Jewish authorities asked Pilate to allow them to break the legs of the men who had been crucified, and to take the bodies down from the crosses. They requested this because it was Friday, and they did not want the bodies to stay on the crosses on the Sabbath, since the coming Sabbath was especially holy. 32 So the soldiers went and broke the legs of the first man and then of the other man who had been crucified with Jesus. 33 But when they came to Jesus, they saw that he was already dead, so they did not break his legs. 34 One of the soldiers, however, plunged his spear into Jesus' side, and at once blood and water poured out. 35 (The one who saw this happen has spoken of it, so that you also may believe.* What he said is true, and he knows

---

19.35 believe; *some manuscripts have* continue to believe.

that he speaks the truth.) 36 This was done to make the scripture come true: "Not one of his bones will be broken." 37 And there is another scripture that says, "People will look at him whom they pierced."

The Burial of Jesus
(Mt 27.57–61; Mk 15.42–47; Lk 23.50–56)

38 After this, Joseph, who was from the town of Arimathea, asked Pilate if he could take Jesus' body. (Joseph was a follower of Jesus, but in secret, because he was afraid of the Jewish authorities.) Pilate told him he could have the body, so Joseph went and took it away. 39 Nicodemus, who at first had gone to see Jesus at night, went with Joseph, taking with him about 30 kilogrammes of spices, a mixture of myrrh and aloes. 40 The two men took Jesus' body and wrapped it in linen with the spices according to the Jewish custom of preparing a body for burial. 41 There was a garden in the place where Jesus had been put to death, and in it there was a new tomb where no one had ever been buried. 42 Since it was the day before the Sabbath and because the tomb was close by, they placed Jesus' body there.

The two men took Jesus' body   (19.40)

The Empty Tomb
(Mt 28.1–8; Mk 16.1–8; Lk 24.1–12)

20 Early on Sunday morning, while it was still dark, Mary Magdalene went to the tomb and saw that the stone had been taken away from the entrance. 2 She went running to

Simon Peter and the other disciple, whom Jesus loved, and told them, "They have taken the Lord from the tomb, and we don't know where they have put him!"

3 Then Peter and the other disciple went to the tomb. 4 The two of them were running, but the other disciple ran faster than Peter and reached the tomb first. 5 He bent over and saw the linen wrappings, but he did not go in. 6 Behind him came Simon Peter, and he went straight into the tomb. He saw the linen wrappings lying there 7 and the cloth which had been round Jesus' head. It was not lying with the linen wrappings but was rolled up by itself. 8 Then the other disciple, who had reached the tomb first, also went in; he saw and believed. 9 (They still did not understand the scripture which said that he must rise from death.) 10 Then the disciples went back home.

Jesus Appears to Mary Magdalene
(Mt 28.9–10; Mk 16.9–11)

11 Mary stood crying outside the tomb. While she was still crying, she bent over and looked in the tomb 12 and saw two angels there dressed in white, sitting where the body of Jesus had been, one at the head and the other at the feet. 13 "Woman, why are you crying?" they asked her.

She answered, "They have taken my Lord away, and I do not know where they have put him!"

14 Then she turned round and saw Jesus standing there; but she did not know that it was Jesus. 15 "Woman, why are you crying?" Jesus asked her. "Who is it that you are looking for?"

She thought he was the gardener, so she said to him, "If you took him away, sir, tell me where you have put him, and I will go and get him."

16 Jesus said to her, "Mary!"

She turned towards him and said in Hebrew, "Rabboni!" (This means "Teacher".)

17 "Do not hold on to me," Jesus told her, "because I have not yet gone back up to the Father. But go to my brothers and tell them that I am returning to him who is my Father and their Father, my God and their God."

18 So Mary Magdalene went and told the disciples that she had seen the Lord and related to them what he had told her.

Jesus Appears to his Disciples
(Mt 28.16–20; Mk 16.14–18; Lk 24.36–49)

19 It was late that Sunday evening, and the disciples were gathered together behind locked doors, because they were afraid of the Jewish authorities. Then Jesus came and stood among them. "Peace be with you," he said. 20 After saying this, he showed them his hands and his side. The disciples were filled with joy at seeing the Lord. 21 Jesus said to them again, "Peace be with you. As the Father sent me, so I send you." 22 Then he breathed on them and said, "Receive the Holy Spirit. 23 If you forgive people's sins, they are forgiven; if you do not forgive them, they are not forgiven."

Jesus came stood among them   (20.19)

Jesus and Thomas

24 One of the twelve disciples, Thomas (called the Twin), was not with them when Jesus came. 25 So the other disciples told him, "We have seen the Lord!"

Thomas said to them, "Unless I see the scars of the nails in his hands and put my finger on those scars and my hand in his side, I will not believe."

26 A week later the disciples were together again indoors, and Thomas was with them. The doors were locked, but Jesus came and stood among them and said, "Peace be with you." 27 Then he said to Thomas, "Put your finger here, and look at my hands;

then stretch out your hand and put it in my side. Stop your doubting, and believe!"

28 Thomas answered him, "My Lord and my God!"

29 Jesus said to him, "Do you believe because you see me? How happy are those who believe without seeing me!"

The Purpose of this Book

30 In his disciples' presence Jesus performed many other miracles which are not written down in this book. 31 But these have been written in order that you may believe* that Jesus is the Messiah, the Son of God, and that through your faith in him you may have life.

Jesus Appears to Seven Disciples

21 After this, Jesus appeared once more to his disciples at Lake Tiberias. This is how it happened. 2 Simon Peter, Thomas (called the Twin), Nathanael (the one from Cana in Galilee), the sons of Zebedee, and two other disciples of Jesus were all together. 3 Simon Peter said to the others, "I am going fishing."

"We will come with you," they told him. So they went out in a boat, but all that night they did not catch a thing. 4 As the sun was rising, Jesus stood at the water's edge, but the disciples did not know that it was Jesus. 5 Then he asked them, "Young men, haven't you caught anything?"

"Not a thing," they answered.

6 He said to them, "Throw your net out on the right side of the boat, and you will catch some." So they threw the net out and could not pull it back in, because they had caught so many fish.

7 The disciple whom Jesus loved said to Peter, "It is the Lord!" When Peter heard that it was the Lord, he wrapped his outer garment round him (for he had taken his clothes off) and jumped into the water. 8 The other disciples came to shore in the boat, pulling the net full of fish. They were not very far from land, about a hundred metres away. 9 When they stepped ashore, they saw a charcoal fire there with fish on it and some bread. 10 Then Jesus said to them, "Bring some of the fish you have just caught."

20.31 believe; *some manuscripts have* continue to believe.

¹¹ Simon Peter went aboard and dragged the net ashore full of big fish, 153 in all; even though there were so many, still the net did not tear. ¹² Jesus said to them, "Come and eat." None of the disciples dared ask him, "Who are you?" because they knew it was the Lord. ¹³ So Jesus went over, took the bread, and gave it to them; he did the same with the fish.

¹⁴ This, then, was the third time Jesus appeared to the disciples after he was raised from death.

Simon Peter ... dragged the net ashore   (21.11)

Jesus and Peter

¹⁵ After they had eaten, Jesus said to Simon Peter, "Simon son of John, do you love me more than these others do?"

"Yes, Lord," he answered, "you know that I love you."

Jesus said to him, "Take care of my lambs." ¹⁶ A second time Jesus said to him, "Simon son of John, do you love me?"

"Yes, Lord," he answered, "you know that I love you."

Jesus said to him, "Take care of my sheep." ¹⁷ A third time Jesus said, "Simon son of John, do you love me?"

Peter was sad because Jesus asked him the third time, "Do you love me?" so he said to him, "Lord, you know everything; you know that I love you!"

Jesus said to him, "Take care of my sheep. ¹⁸ I am telling you the truth: when you were young, you used to get ready and go anywhere you wanted to; but when you are old, you will stretch out your hands and someone else will bind you and take you where you don't want to go." 19 (In saying this, Jesus was indicating the way in which Peter would die and bring glory to God.) Then Jesus said to him, "Follow me!"

Jesus and the Other Disciple

20 Peter turned round and saw behind him that other disciple, whom Jesus loved — the one who had leaned close to Jesus at the meal and had asked, "Lord, who is going to betray you?" 21 When Peter saw him, he asked Jesus, "Lord, what about this man?"

22 Jesus answered him, "If I want him to live until I come, what is that to you? Follow me!"

23 So a report spread among the followers of Jesus that this disciple would not die. But Jesus did not say that he would not die; he said, "If I want him to live until I come, what is that to you?"

24 He is the disciple who spoke of these things, the one who also wrote them down; and we know that what he said is true.

Conclusion

25 Now, there are many other things that Jesus did. If they were all written down one by one, I suppose that the whole world could not hold the books that would be written.